Earth's oceans

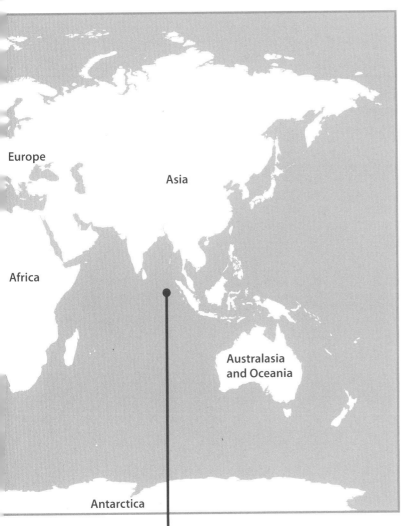

Europe

Asia

Africa

Australasia and Oceania

Antarctica

Atlantic Ocean

The second-largest ocean is also the saltiest. The Atlantic Ocean forms an S-shape as it divides North and South America from Europe and Africa.

Area: 106.5 million sq km (41.1 million sq miles)

Average depth: 3,646 m (11,960 ft)

Climate: Mild and stormy

Southern Ocean

Bordering Antarctica, the Southern Ocean has cold and windy waters. Icebergs break off from the continent's huge ice sheets and float away into the ocean.

Area: 20.3 million sq km (7.9 million sq miles)

Average depth: 4,500 m (14,800 ft)

Climate: Cold and stormy

Indian Ocean

The world's warmest ocean is the Indian Ocean. It has many trade routes connecting the Middle East and Africa with Oceania and the Americas.

Area: 70.6 million sq km (27.2 million sq miles)

Average depth: 3,960 m (12,990 ft)

Climate: Hot and humid

Things to find out:

DKfindout!

Oceans

Author: Andrea Mills

Editorial assistant Katie Lawrence
Project editor Radhika Haswani
Senior editor Roohi Sehgal
Project art editors Emma Hobson, Rashika Kachroo
Senior art editor Nidhi Mehra
DTP designers Sachin Gupta, Vijay Kandwal
Project picture researcher Sakshi Saluja
Jacket co-ordinator Issy Walsh
Jacket designer Rashika Kachroo
Jacket editor Radhika Haswani
Managing editors Jonathan Melmoth, Monica Saigal
Managing art editors Diane Peyton Jones,
Romi Chakraborty
Senior producer, pre-production Jennifer Murray
Producer, pre-production Heather Blagden
Senior producer Ena Matagic
Delhi team head Malavika Talukder
Creative directors Clare Baggaley, Helen Senior
Publishing director Sarah Larter

Subject consultant Dr Jonathan Dale
Educational consultant Jacqueline Harris

First published in Great Britain in 2020
by Dorling Kindersley Limited
One Embassy Gardens, 8 Viaduct Gardens, London, SW11 7BW

A CIP catalogue record for this book
is available from the British Library.
ISBN: 978-0-2414-4279-1

Printed and bound in China

A WORLD OF IDEAS:
SEE ALL THERE IS TO KNOW

www.dk.com

Contents

Spiny lobster

Dumbo octopus

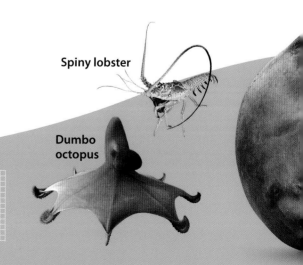

The scale boxes on pages 16–17 and
42–43 of this book show you how big
an animal is compared to a person
or a diver who is 1.8 m (6 ft) tall.

» Scale

Arctic tern

Tabular iceberg

Puffin

Northern
elephant seal

Starfish

What is an ocean?

Oceans are the largest bodies of water on Earth. These huge, underwater habitats are home to millions of different types of plants and animals. Oceans are salty because when water evaporates into the air it leaves behind salt.

Deep blue sea
Bright sunshine makes clear seawater look blue. This is because water can absorb, or take in, all the colours in sunlight except blue, which is reflected instead.

Seas and lakes

The main differences between seas and lakes are their size and saltiness. Seas are bigger and saltier than lakes. Lakes almost always have fresh water, which is not salty.

Seas are smaller than oceans, but are connected to them. There are many more seas than oceans. Almost all of our seas are salt water.

Mediterranean Sea by Sardinia, Italy

Salt lakes

A few lakes are salty. Water flows into these lakes from surrounding rivers, but does not flow out. Instead, water evaporates from these lakes and leaves behind salt. The Dead Sea in the Middle East and the Great Salt Lake in the USA are both lakes that contain salt water instead of fresh water.

Great Salt Lake
The Great Salt Lake is about five times saltier than the oceans.

Dead Sea
The Dead Sea is almost 10 times saltier than the oceans.

Lake Kivu, Rwanda

Lakes are similar to giant ponds, and are completely surrounded by land. They contain fresh water, which comes from nearby streams or rivers.

! WOW!

We know more about the surface of the **Moon** than the **bottom** of the **oceans.**

How are oceans formed?

Our planet is a wonderfully watery world. Oceans cover more than 70 per cent of Earth's surface, and contain 97 per cent of the total water supply on Earth. The oceans formed almost 4 billion years ago, when low-lying areas became filled with rainwater.

Moving plates

Earth's surface is mad up of a thin crust, whi covers the top of the h rocky mantle. Togethe the crust and mantle make moving pieces of land, called tectoni plates. Where these pla pull apart, new ocean floor develops.

Making waves

Ocean waves are influenced by wind speed, distance, and direction. Their size and shape range from tiny ripples to giant swells.

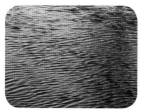

Ripple
A gentle wind blowing over the ocean results in small ripples.

Chop
Stronger winds make rough waves known as chops.

Swell
Large waves, known as swells, create a more regular wave pattern over time.

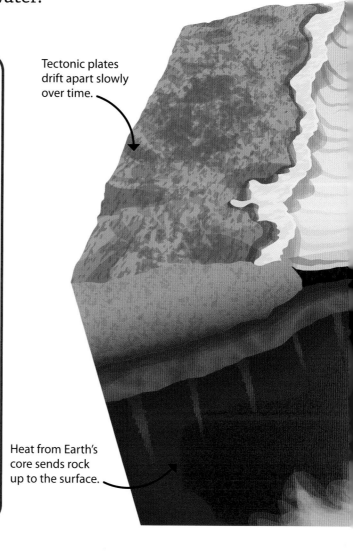

Tectonic plates drift apart slowly over time.

Heat from Earth's core sends rock up to the surface.

Seawater covers much of planet Earth

Rain clouds build up before a downpour

bal ocean

en Earth first developed, its surface was almost entirely
an. As the first continents formed, water in hollow
as became the five oceans we know today.

Water vapour

In the past, oceans were formed when hot
gases were released from under Earth's
surface. These gases cooled to become water
vapour. The vapour turned into water droplets,
which gathered as heavy rain clouds in the sky.

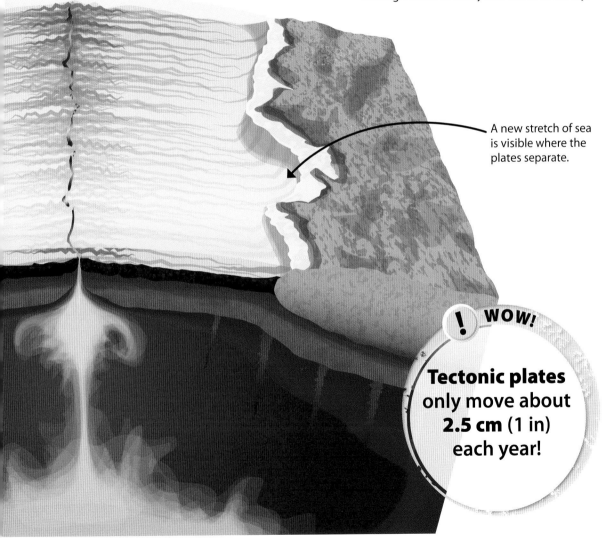

A new stretch of sea
is visible where the
plates separate.

! WOW!

Tectonic plates
only move about
2.5 cm (1 in)
each year!

A drop in the ocean

The world's seven continents are surrounded by water. The Pacific Ocean is the largest ocean, and it covers around a third of the planet's surface. The Arctic Ocean is the smallest and coldest ocean – it has sea ice all year round.

Key to oceans and seas

A	Pacific Ocean
B	Arctic Ocean
C	Southern Ocean
D	Atlantic Ocean
E	Indian Ocean
F	Arabian Sea
G	Red Sea
H	Mediterranean Sea
I	Adriatic Sea
J	Black Sea
K	Persian Gulf
L	Baltic Sea
M	North Sea
N	Caribbean Sea

B

North America

A

N

D

South America

Blue planet

Earth is known as the blue planet because it is mostly covered in water. This is almost all salt water, which is found in the five main oceans and many smaller seas. Only a small amount of Earth's water is drinkable fresh water, which lies in lakes and rivers.

Antarctica

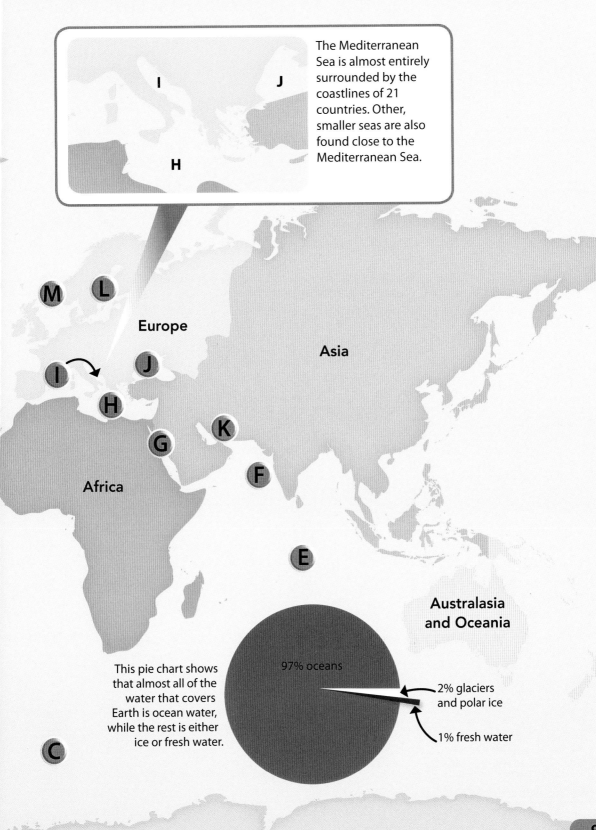

The Mediterranean Sea is almost entirely surrounded by the coastlines of 21 countries. Other, smaller seas are also found close to the Mediterranean Sea.

Europe

Asia

Africa

Australasia and Oceania

This pie chart shows that almost all of the water that covers Earth is ocean water, while the rest is either ice or fresh water.

97% oceans

2% glaciers and polar ice

1% fresh water

Ocean zones

Sunlight sparkles on the surface of the oceans, lighting up sea creatures swimming in shallow waters. Deep down on the sea bed it is another story. There is constant darkness, falling temperatures, and very little sea life. Oceans can be divided into five zones, which relate to the conditions at different depths.

! WOW!

Some oceans are more than **10 km (6 miles) deep.**

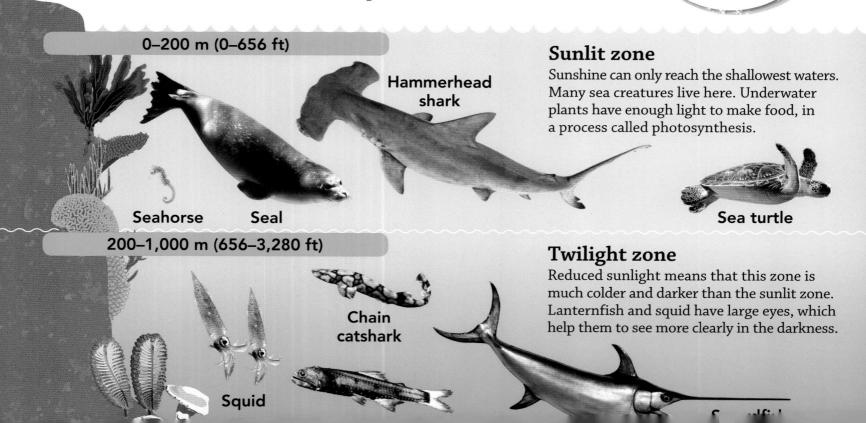

0–200 m (0–656 ft)

Hammerhead shark

Seahorse   **Seal**

Sea turtle

Sunlit zone

Sunshine can only reach the shallowest waters. Many sea creatures live here. Underwater plants have enough light to make food, in a process called photosynthesis.

200–1,000 m (656–3,280 ft)

Chain catshark

Squid

Twilight zone

Reduced sunlight means that this zone is much colder and darker than the sunlit zone. Lanternfish and squid have large eyes, which help them to see more clearly in the darkness.

Midnight zone

This zone is in total darkness. Huge pressure comes from the heavy water above, but some creatures, such as jellyfish, have soft bodies, which stop them being crushed.

Footballfish

Tiburonia jellyfish

Frilled shark

Dumbo octopus

4,000–6,000 m (13,123–19,685 ft)

Abyss

Meaning "bottomless" in Greek, the abyss is freezing cold. The amount of water above it means that this zone has a level of pressure that is hundreds of times greater than on the surface.

Sea pig

Hagfish

Tripod fish

Below 6,000 m (19,685 ft)

Hadal

The deepest and darkest depths of the ocean in the hadal zone are almost empty. Food is in short supply, so sea creatures down here eat bacteria and waste material, which falls to the ocean floor.

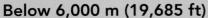

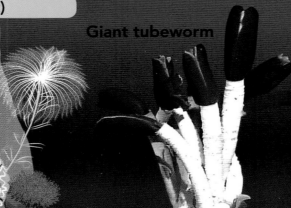

Giant tubeworm

Bioluminescent fish

Some creatures in the deeper zones have adapted to the darkness by using chemicals in their bodies to create their own light – this is called bioluminescence. Glowing in the dark allows them to recognize each other, catch prey, and scare away predators.

Brilliant bioluminescent jellyfish

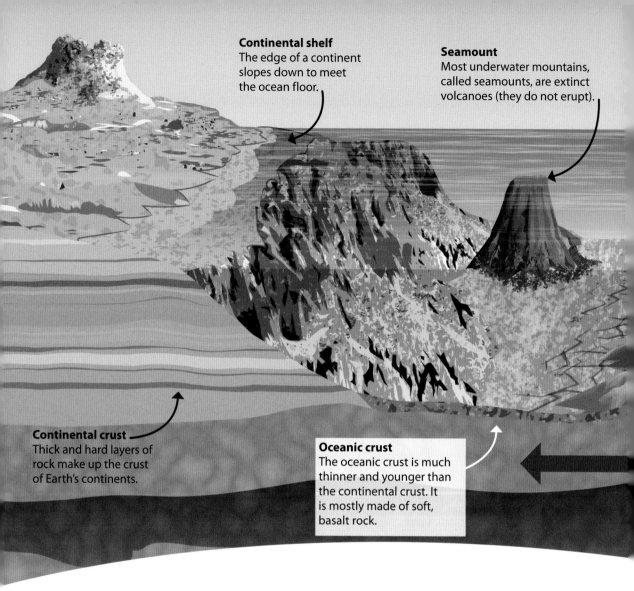

Continental shelf
The edge of a continent slopes down to meet the ocean floor.

Seamount
Most underwater mountains, called seamounts, are extinct volcanoes (they do not erupt).

Continental crust
Thick and hard layers of rock make up the crust of Earth's continents.

Oceanic crust
The oceanic crust is much thinner and younger than the continental crust. It is mostly made of soft, basalt rock.

Ocean floor

Journeying down to the ocean floor reveals a fascinating underwater landscape. This bumpy sea bed has many similar features to dry land. There are steep slopes, deep cracks, and rising mountains. But there is one big difference – there's no light down here.

! WOW!

The **Ring of Fire** in the Pacific Ocean has more than **450 volcanoes**.

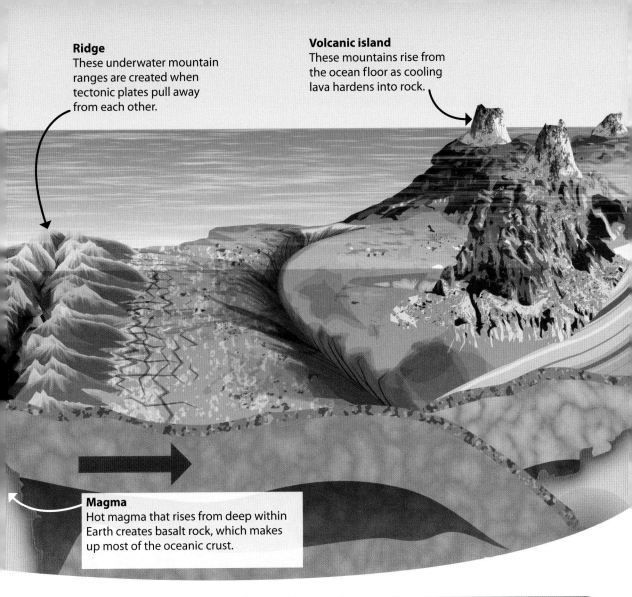

Ridge
These underwater mountain ranges are created when tectonic plates pull away from each other.

Volcanic island
These mountains rise from the ocean floor as cooling lava hardens into rock.

Magma
Hot magma that rises from deep within Earth creates basalt rock, which makes up most of the oceanic crust.

Limited life

Not many creatures can survive in the darkest depths of the ocean. Those that do, rely on chemicals instead of light to make their food. Sea life develops around hot springs on the ocean floor, where the water is full of minerals.

Hydrothermal vent
Deep-sea vents release extremely hot water from deep in Earth.

Sea anemones
These creatures cover themselves in sand for protection.

Tubeworms
Giant tubeworms eat the tiny bacteria that grow near hydrothermal vents.

Frozen features

The Arctic and Antarctica are among the most remote, or hard to get to, places on Earth. The Arctic is a freezing cold region that is mostly sea. Antarctica is a continent almost completely covered by ice. Very low temperatures affect these places and transform their landscapes.

Ice shelves attached to the Antarctic coastline

Ice shelves

Most ice shelves are found in Antarctica. These giant platforms form where a glacier or ice sheet moves slowly down to the coastline. Antarctica's record-breaking Ross Ice Shelf is about the same size as France!

An iceberg floating along a strip of sea in Greenland

Icebergs

When great chunks of ice break off from a glacier or ice sheet, they float out to sea as icebergs. Less than 20 per cent of the total iceberg is visible above the surface of the water.

Plankton bloom

Summer sunlight melts some of the sea ice, allowing tiny sea life to develop. In polar regions, small plants called phytoplankton grow rapidly, which causes a bloom. This bloom provides a much-needed source of food for sea creatures.

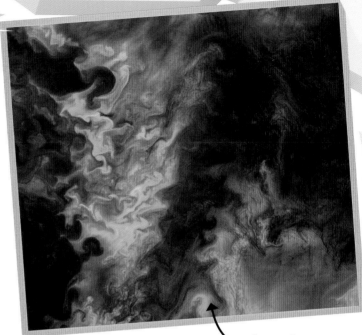

This satellite image shows an enormous phytoplankton bloom.

Frozen food

The Southern Ocean is home to a huge amount of Antarctic krill. These small creatures are at the heart of the marine food chain. Krill feed on phytoplankton, but they are eaten by whales, seals, and penguins.

Life on the ice

Life is tough by the oceans in the North and South poles. The freezing conditions mean that many animals struggle to survive. While some travel to warmer places to escape the cold, those left behind must adapt to the temperature and lack of food.

FACT FILE

»» **Length:** Up to 3 m (10 ft)

»» **Weight:** Up to 600 kg (1,320 lb)

»» **Swim speed:** Up to 39 kph (24 mph)

»» **Ocean:** Southern

Leopard seal

A double layer of fat keeps seals warm. The leopard seal's smooth body shape is suited to fast swimming, while its powerful jaws are used to catch prey.

»» Scale

FACT FILE

»» **Height:** Up to 0.8 m (2.5 ft)

»» **Weight:** Up to 5.4 kg (12 lb)

»» **Swim speed:** Up to 36 kph (22 mph)

»» **Ocean:** Southern

»» Scale

»» Scale

FACT FILE

»» **Height:** Up to 1.2 m (4 ft)

»» **Weight:** Up to 40 kg (88 lb)

»» **Swim speed:** Up to 12 kph (8 mph)

»» **Ocean:** Southern

Gentoo penguin

To stay warm and active, penguins have thick skin and layers of fat, called blubber. With their wing-like flippers, they can swim at high speeds to catch fish.

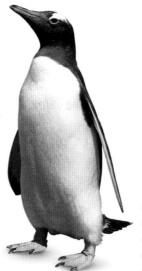

Emperor pengui

This, the tallest and heaviest penguin, has many feathers and layers of fat to help keep it warm. Emperor penguins also huddle up in groups to stay warm.

lar bear

...o coats of fur and layers of ...help the largest predator ...land survive the Arctic's ...ezing conditions. Black ...n under the polar bear's ...absorbs heat from ... Sun.

White fur is the perfect camouflage. It helps polar bears to blend in with the surrounding snow and ice.

FACT FILE

» **Height:** Up to 1.5 m (5 ft)

» **Weight:** Up to 800 kg (1,764 lb)

» **Swim speed:** Up to 10 kph (6 mph)

» **Ocean:** Arctic

» Scale

FACT FILE

〉 **Length:** Up to ...5 m (11.5 ft)

〉 **Weight:** Up to ...,800 kg (3,968 lb)

〉 **Swim speed:** Up to ...5 kph (21 mph)

〉 **Ocean:** Arctic

» Scale

Walrus

These huge, blubbery mammals use their large tusks as weapons when defending their land. Their fat stores keep them warm.

...rca

...ten known as the killer whale, this speedy, ...ubbery swimmer uses its flippers and the ...n on top of its body, called the dorsal fin, ...glide through the water.

...cale

Orcas travel in groups, called pods, to keep each other warm.

FACT FILE

» **Length:** Up to 10 m (32 ft)

» **Weight:** Up to 6,600 kg (14,550 lb)

» **Swim speed:** Up to 56 kph (35 mph)

» **Ocean:** Arctic and Southern

Icebergs

Giant blocks of frozen ice float through the coldest waters on Earth. They were once attached to glaciers or ice sheets, but these icebergs have broken off and drifted away, in a process called calving. Most icebergs are found in Antarctica and the North Atlantic Ocean.

Islands of ice

A piece of ice must measure more than 30 m (100 ft) wide and 5 m (16 ft) above sea level to be called an iceberg. The biggest icebergs can be as large as a small country!

Tabular icebergs always have a flat top and steep sides.

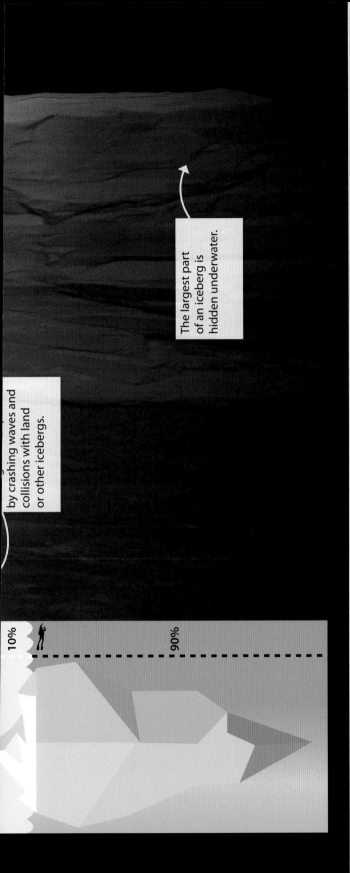

by crashing waves and collisions with land or other icebergs.

The largest part of an iceberg is hidden underwater.

10%

90%

Iceberg types

Icebergs are grouped together by shape. Tabular icebergs are the most common, but non-tabular types can be many different shapes.

An iceberg with a slope on one side and a steep cliff on the other is called a wedge.

Wedge

U-shaped

An iceberg may be eroded (gradually worn away) over time to form an arch.

Pinnacle

This type of iceberg has at least one tall column.

Shipwrecks

Ships destroyed at sea can be lost forever, or left untouched as watery graves. Whether caused by natural disasters or warfare, shipwrecks help us find out about the history of sinking ships and sailors who died at sea. Their discoveries reveal stories just waiting to be told...

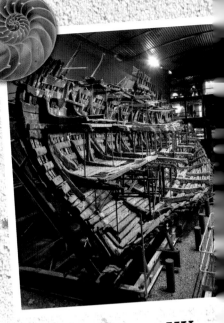

Mary Rose, UK

One of English King Henry VI[I]
largest warships, the *Mary R[ose]*
sank during a sea battle in 15[__]
and hundreds of people die[d]
Raised from the ocean floor [in]
1982, what is left of the ship [can]
be seen in Portsmouth, UK

Vasa, Sweden

Doomed from the start, the 17th-century warship *Vasa* had a leak and sank on its first trip, in 1628, just 1.3 km (0.8 miles) after leaving Stockholm, Sweden. Finally recovered in 1961, the ship is now on display in Sweden.

RMS *Titanic*, UK

Even though it was launched as an "unsinkable ship", RMS *Titanic* sank in 1912 on its first journey after hitting an iceberg in the Atlantic Ocean. Hundreds of people died, as there were not enough lifeboats on the ship.

SS *Central America*, USA

This steam-powered ship sailed between Central America and the USA until a hurricane destroyed it in 1857. Nicknamed the "Ship of Gold", it sank with a stash of gold worth about £1.5 million ($2 million) at the time.

weepstakes, Canada

weepstakes lies in shallow aters off the coast of Ontario, anada. This ship hit a rock ear Cove Island, Canada, n 1885 and sank before he damage could be fixed. oday, divers can explore he underwater wreck.

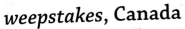

MS *World Discoverer*, Germany

German cruise ship MS *World Discoverer* travelled the world until it hit a reef and got stuck in shallow waters in the South Pacific in 2000. Luckily, everyone on board escaped, but the ship remains on its side to this day.

Ocean homes

The world's waters offer a variety of homes and hideaways for different sea creatures. With many types of natural resources in ocean habitats all over the world, ocean dwellers use plants, rock, and coral to make safe shelters or create camouflage.

A sea lion swims in the kelp forests of California, USA.

Kelp forests

These underwater forests of giant seaweed are home to creatures big and small, from sea lions and whales to sea urchins and tiny fish. The kelp seaweed doubles up as a source of food and a protective shelter.

Mangroves

These swamplands provide coastal homes for marine life. The mixture of mineral-rich waters, plenty of food, twisting tree roots, and shallow waters suits fish, crabs, shrimps, oysters, snails, and sponges. Many fish raise their young in mangroves.

A saltwater crocodile is hard to spot in a mangrove forest in Sri Lanka.

Shells

Some marine creatures use sea shells as body armour. Hermit crabs can make new homes in the empty shells of sea snails. These crabs even carry the shells around the sea bed with them!

Sea turtle swimming through a coral reef

Red hermit crab making a snail shell into a new home

Corals

Colourful coral is an underwater playground for clownfish, seahorses, and sea turtles. Some sea snails attach coral to their shells for camouflage.

Rocky crevices

Hidden among shadowy rocks are crevices, or narrow cracks. Sea urchins, sea stars, sea cucumbers, barnacles, spider crabs, and anemones use the darkness in these cracks to lie low and avoid predators.

Spiky sea urchins gather in groups next to the rocks.

Seagrasses are a comfortable habitat for sea stars.

Seagrasses

These flowering plants provide hundreds of types of sea creatures with a place to live. While sea stars and sea urchins live among the long grasses, manatees and sea turtles eat these plants.

Fish food

The ocean food chain shows us who eats what in the underwater world. The tiniest creatures are producers – they make plant and animal food. Larger fish and mammals are consumers – they hunt prey to eat.

Phytoplankton

Tiny algae called phytoplankton are the biggest producer of food in the oceans. Phytoplankton sit at the very bottom of the food chain. They create essential food supplies for small marine animals.

Arctic tern

Seabirds

Together with seals, seabirds are the main consumers of salmonidae. They swoop down to the surface of the ocean and pluck fish out of the water.

Harbour seal

Sharks

The top predators in the ocean food chain are sharks. These skilled hunters target a range of prey, including seals, dolphins, turtles, seabirds, and fish.

Seals

Seals have big appetites. Their seafood diet includes fish, octopus, and squid. However, seals must always stay alert to the threat of a shark or polar bear attack.

Tiger shark

Zooplankton

The main consumers of phytoplankton are zooplankton. These tiny animals include the Antarctic krill, which are small, shrimp-like creatures that grow up to only 6.5 cm (2.5 in) long.

Antarctic krill

Forage fish

Small forage fish, such as the colourful goldband fusilier, feast on zooplankton. These fish are an important part of the food chain as they are the main source of food for many larger creatures.

Goldband fusilier

Salmonidae

Animals get bigger as they get higher up the food chain. This group of large fish, which includes salmon and trout, are hunters. They feed on forage fish and marine insects.

Brook trout

Polar bears

At home on the Arctic sea ice, polar bears are hunters who are always on the lookout for a tasty seal. When seals are in short supply, they will feed on the carcasses (dead bodies) of whales.

Defence mechanisms

Ocean predators had better watch out! Their prey are finding more and more inventive ways to avoid attack and protect themselves. Whether blending into the background to hide from hunters or fighting back with weapons, these sea creatures are not going down without a fight.

Sting in the tail

The blue-spotted stingray would rather swim away than fight, so its bright, blue spots warn predators to back off. If it is attacked, the spiky stinger on its tail releases a deadly poison.

Poisonous spines

Deadly lionfish have poisonous spines that can kill other marine life and also paralyse humans. Their colourful spines can be clearly seen, and are a warning to predators to stay back.

Camouflage

The marine master of disguise is the cuttlefish. It can change its appearance very quickly. The cuttlefish can make its skin colour and texture blend so well wit its surroundings that predators can't see i

fety in numbers

h swim in groups called shoals,
cause it reduces the likelihood
being attacked. Predators can
overwhelmed by large shoals
d struggle to pick a single target.

Puffing up

The porcupine fish scares off predators
by sucking in water to look bigger.
An inflated porcupine fish is almost
impossible for predators to eat.

Cloud of ink

Like a marine magician, the common
octopus can do a disappearing act. If
predators come close, it releases a cloud
of dark ink to hide itself and create a
diversion before making its escape.

Ocean hunters

Predators in water develop special skills, which help them catch prey. Some have sharpened senses that pick out a target in the darkness. Others rely on a sleek, streamlined shape to move quickly through the water when giving chase. In the final attack, those who have strong jaws and sharp teeth ensure a deadly outcome.

Sea urchins

These spiky sea creatures cannot swim, so instead they have stinging spines, which the use for self-defence. Their beak-like mouths help them to scrape dead fish, mussels, and algae from underwater rocks to eat.

Swordfish

Built for speed, the streamlined swordfish one of the ocean's largest predators. The have special organs that heat up their eyes for better underwater vision, while their "sword" is used to knock out prey.

The swordfish's "sword" also pushes water aside for high-speed hunting.

Wolffish

Beware the Atlantic wolffish! This fearsome predator has wolf-like fangs and an eel-like body, which reaches up to 1.5 m (5 ft) long. They like to eat sea urchins and crabs, but wolffish will also attack people!

Dahlia anemones

This creature looks like a pretty flower growing on ocean rocks, but it is really a deadly predator. Its many tentacles trap prey, and they have stinging tips, which are used to kill marine life.

JELLYFISH

These deadly hunters are found all over the world. Anything that comes into contact with their long tentacles receives a poisonous sting. This paralyses prey (stops it moving), which is then ready for the jellyfish to eat.

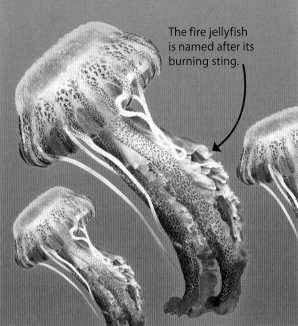

The fire jellyfish is named after its burning sting.

Ribbon eels

s predator looks like a colourful ribbon
n swimming through the water. Its
trils detect the vibrations of nearby fish,
n the eel moves in to catch its prey
n strong jaws and sharp teeth.

Blacktip reef sharks

imming along tropical coastlines and coral reefs, these sharks find
ength in numbers. They hunt in small groups to increase their threat,
ore they sink their jagged teeth with ease into their prey.

Dangerous waters

The ocean can be a dangerous and even deadly place. Extreme weather and underwater activity can make powerful winds, huge waves, and raging storms. Seas and coastlines can suddenly turn into disaster zones, with widespread destruction and loss of life.

! **WOW!**

Tsunamis can travel at speeds of up to **805 kph (500 mph).**

Cyclones

Strong, twisting winds reaching up to 300 kph (185 mph) can develop quickly in tropical waters. They form in extreme heat, when the sea temperature rises above 26°C (78°F). Cyclones are also called typhoons in some parts of the world.

Floods

If rivers burst their banks, the flood water can wash away buildings, people, and animals. When huge storms cause sea levels to rise near coastlines, coastal flooding can occur.

Whirlpools

At the point where different currents meet, a spiral of swirling water sometimes develops. This is called a whirlpool. Most are weak, but some are powerful and are known as maelstroms. Their strong spin can pull swimmers and boats underwater.

Volcanoes

Most active underwater volcanoes are found at the edge of tectonic plates. These hot spots cause Earth's crust to split, which releases lava and volcanic ash. Water cools the lava and ash, creating hard rocks known as pillow lava.

Tsunamis

The sudden motion of an earthquake or volcano can lead to giant waves of water, known as tsunamis. The shockwaves caused when part of the sea bed moves can create a series of fast waves travelling towards the coastline.

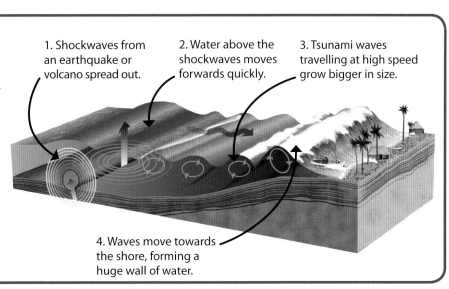

1. Shockwaves from an earthquake or volcano spread out.

2. Water above the shockwaves moves forwards quickly.

3. Tsunami waves travelling at high speed grow bigger in size.

4. Waves move towards the shore, forming a huge wall of water.

Ocean motion

Swimming is the main type of underwater travel, but not all sea creatures are built for swimming. Instead, their body shapes are better suited to other forms of transport, such as going with the flow of the water or catching a ride with another animal!

Swish, swish!

Swim
Sharks have long fins that keep them afloat, huge, streamlined bodies, and swishing tails to swim quickly through the water. Their dorsal fins keep them upright.

Afloat
The nautilus lives inside one chamber of its outer shell. The other chambers fill with gas and water to stop the nautilus from sinking.

Drift
With no way of moving by itself, the Portuguese man-of-war drifts along on the ocean current, trailing poisonous tentacles behind it.

Dive and steer

Seals dive deep underwater. Their two front flippers are used for steering, while two back flippers propel the seal forwards.

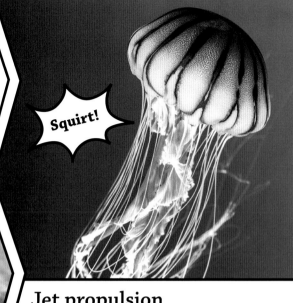

Squirt!

Jet propulsion

Jellyfish move using jet propulsion. They open and squeeze their bodies to blast out jets of water and move in the right direction.

Woohoo!

Barnacles underneath a sea turtle

Leap

Dolphins are graceful swimmers. Sometimes, they use their torpedo-shaped bodies to build up enough speed to leap out of the water.

Hitch a ride

Baby barnacles pick a spot and attach themselves to it forever. This could be a rock, a boat, or even a passing sea turtle!

Seabirds

Soaring over the open ocean, seabirds are fantastic fliers who can stay away from land for years at a time. Many live together along coastlines, in groups called colonies, and hunt for fish. They have webbed feet, waterproof feathers, and organs that control their salt levels – three key features that help them thrive by the sea.

Albatross

Measuring up to 3.5 m (12 ft) wide, the albatross has the largest wingspan of any bird. These giant wings help the bird glide over water for a long time in search of food. Its hooked beak helps the albatross keep hold of slippery fish.

Pelican

By diving underwater or dipping its big beak under the water's surface, the pelican can catch lots of fish. Then, it stores the fish in its stretchy mouth pouch, which can hold three times more fish than its stomach.

Feeding flocks

A good food supply can mean that huge numbers of birds gather together. Flamingos live in flocks, or groups, of up to a million birds. Their beaks work like sieves, filtering out shrimps from the water. These shrimps give flamingos their famous pink colour.

Flamingos flocking together to find food

Guillemot

Cliffside colonies are home to large numbers of guillemots. Their feathers act as camouflage, as they have dark backs and white fronts to match the cliffs. Guillemots are skilled divers and can plunge up to 180 m (590 ft) into the sea to catch fish.

Puffin

Rocky islands are perfect homes for puffins. Their large, webbed feet and short, fin-like wings mean they can swim fast to find food. The puffin's colourful beak has spikes, so it can hold many fish at once.

Island hotspots

Hot magma from inside the Earth can melt down the thin oceanic crust and break through to the surface. These areas are known as hotspots. As the magma rises higher, it forms an underwater volcano. Repeated eruptions of magma can spread out to form groups of volcanic islands.

The coastline on Kilauea volcano

FACT FILE

» **Location:** Central Pacific Ocean

» **Nationality:** American

» **Language:** Hawaiian, English

Hawaii

The Hawaiian Islands dotted across 2,700 (1,700 miles) of the Pacific Ocean. They formed as the ocean floor moved slowly o a hotspot. The Hawa volcano Kilauea is the world's most active volcano. It has been continuously eruptin since 1983.

Iceland

This beautiful island developed from eruptions on the underwater Mid-Ocean Ridge mountain chain millions of years ago. Iceland is one of the only places where the ocean ridge is dry land.

FACT FILE

» **Location:** North Atlantic Ocean

» **Nationality:** Icelandic

» **Language:** Icelandic

Iceland has about 30 active volcanoes.

Galápagos

Known for their unique wildlife, the 21 volcanic islands of Galápagos formed from a hotspot in the East Pacific Ocean. The youngest volcanoes on the Fernandina and Isabela islands are still erupting.

The volcanic islands of Galápagos

Réunion

This island formed over a hotspot in the Indian Ocean around 5 million years ago. One of the volcanoes on Réunion Island, Piton de la Fournaise, erupts regularly.

Cirque de Salazie volcano in Réunion

Easter Island

Easter Island was formed from a hotspot in the Pacific Ocean around 750,000 years ago. This island is 1,700 km (1,100 miles) away from its closest neighbour. Ancient Polynesians used the volcanic rock on the island to create head statues, called moai.

The moai statues of Easter Island

Coral reefs

Even though coral reefs cover less than
1 per cent of our oceans, they are home
to 25 per cent of all sea life! These huge
rocky structures grow gradually from the
skeletons of tiny sea creatures. Animals
and plants find shelter and safety here,
turning reefs into underwater worlds
of spectacular colour.

Great Barrier Reef
Australia's Great Barrier Reef
started growing about 8,000 years
ago. Today, it is the world's largest
reef, covering 344,400 sq km
(132,900 sq miles) and it is
even visible from space.

Fire coral growing off the coast of Egypt

Red Sea reefs
The crystal clear waters of the Red Sea reefs, in the Middle East, are an oasis for snorkellers and divers, who go to see the colourful corals and amazing variety of fish.

The Great Blue Hole

Turtles are often seen at Apo

Lighthouse Reef
This reef in the Caribbean Sea is best known for its Great Blue Hole. This is a chasm, or a very deep hole, which resulted from the collapse of an underwater cave.

Apo Reef
The largest reef in the Philippines is located in the Apo Reef Natural Park. Many people come here to swim with giant sea turtles.

Pickles Reef
Many underwater photographers travel to this small reef in the Florida Keys, USA, because of its eye-catching coral and warm waters.

Shoals of fish caught on camera

Giants of the ocean

Among the ocean's best-known animals are sharks, whales, and dolphins. These groups are some of the largest creatures on Earth. They share many of the same features, which help them breathe, feed, and swim underwater. Whales and dolphins are sea mammals, but sharks are fish.

Spinner dolphin

Dorsal fin
Fish and sea mammals have a dorsal fin on their backs to stay upright in the water. This keeps them stable when swimming, and helps them to change direction smoothly.

Cat shark

Bottlenose dolphin

Tail
Powerful tails can push large sea creatures through the water. The tails of whales and dolphins go up and down, while the tails of sharks go from side to side.

Body
Sharks and dolphins have streamlined shapes and smooth bodies, which are suited to swimming. Torpedo-shaped dolphins can leap out of the water!

Great white shark

Narwhal

ead

ost sharks, whales, and dolphins
ve rounded, streamlined heads. The
eat white shark is easily recognized
its huge jaws and sharp teeth,
ich are ready to tear into prey.

Horn

At home in Arctic waters,
the narwhal stands out
among other sea mammals
as it has a large, sword-like
horn. This horn is really a
long tooth, which detects
changes in the surroundings.

Whopper whale

The biggest creature on Earth is the blue
whale. Measuring up to 30 m (100 ft)
long and weighing 150 tonnes (165 tons),
this mighty mammal has a heart the
same size as a small car.

Bryde's whale

Underbelly

Whales are covered in
a layer of blubber (fat)
up to 15 cm (6 in) thick.
Their underbellies hold
huge amounts of food,
and have more than one
stomach to digest it.

Marine migrators

Some sea creatures journey far and wide just to survive. They travel huge distances across the oceans searching for food, or a safe place to rest and breed. These regular group movements are called migrations.

Blue marlin

Among the world's fastest fish, blue marlin reach top speeds of 80 kph (50 mph). They travel hundreds of kilometres to find food and warm waters.

» Scale

The blue marlin's streamlined body is bright blue on top and white underneath.

Northern elephant seal

This seal travels 21,000 km (13,000 miles) to find prey to eat. It returns to the same places every year.

» Scale

Its huge, blubbery body can survive without food for months at a time.

Leatherback turtle

The largest type of sea turtle travels between its breeding and feeding grounds. It covers distances of more than 16,000 km (10,000 miles) a year.

» Scale

This turtle has soft, leather-like skin on its back instead of a hard shell.

Two long antennae help the spiny lobster fight off predators.

Spiny lobster

These lobsters migrate in large groups in search of coral reefs. During their migration, they travel in long, neat lines along the sea bed.

» Scale

» Scale

Humpback whale

These massive mammals can be 18 m (60 ft) long. The distance between their breeding and feeding grounds reaches 5,000 km (3,100 miles).

Humpback whales can weigh up to 40 tonnes (44 tons), which is around 60 times heavier than a cow!

JACQUES COUSTEAU

French explorer Jacques Cousteau (1910–1997) designed and built scuba devices, diving saucers, and underwater work stations for scientists. His own deep-sea dives were caught on camera in films and television series.

Cousteau on board one of his diving saucers

SYLVIA EARLE

American oceanographer Sylvia Earle (1935–present) built special diving equipment to discover new marine life and ocean features. She is committed to protecting the oceans and launched Mission Blue – an organization that creates marine-protected areas around the world.

Earle showing her deep-sea exploration vehicle

Underwater explorers

The oceans remained a mystery until the 19th century, when underwater exploration began. The invention of submersibles (underwater vehicles) allowed scientists to visit the deepest seas. Their research opened up the oceans as never before, but even today, only five per cent of the world's waters have been explored.

JACQUES PICCARD

Swiss submarine fan Jacques Piccard (1922–2008) designed underwater vehicles to explore the oceans. In 1960, he climbed aboard his father's bathyscaphe (a type of submersible) *Trieste*, and went down to the deepest point on Earth – the Mariana Trench in the Pacific Ocean.

One of Piccard's submarines in 1980

CINDY LEE VAN DOVER

American ocean explorer Cindy Lee Van Dover (1954–present) is the only female pilot of the deep-sea diving submersible *Alvin*. She found many giant tubeworms and hydrothermal vents during about 50 journeys underwater.

Alvin, the deep-sea ocean research submersible

Underwater work

There are many different career options for people who enjoy the oceans. Some of these jobs involve studying marine life, researching ocean features, and protecting the waters.

Marine biologist
Researchers of ocean habitats and marine life

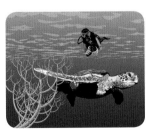

Underwater photographer
Scuba divers who record underwater action

Marine archaeology
The study of ocean history, such as shipwrecks

Aquatic veterinarian
Vets who specialize in treating marine animals

Ocean exploration

Thanks to improvements in marine technology and equipment, people can explore more of the oceans than ever before. Basic breathing equipment allows for snorkelling near the surface, while more complicated underwater vehicles can visit the deepest sea bed.

Scuba diving

Scuba divers are equipped with an oxygen tank, so that they can breathe underwater. Increased interest in scuba diving has led to discoveries of ancient cities and shipwrecks, as well as encounters with mysterious marine life.

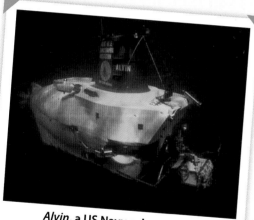

Alvin, a US Navy submersible

Diving regulator
This controls pressure inside the oxygen tank to make it suitable for breathing.

Weight belt
This belt has lead weights, which keep scuba divers underwater.

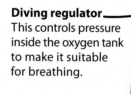

Deep-diving submersibles

The deepest depths can only be explored by sturdy submersibles (underwater vehicles) that can cope with high water pressure. Scientists use submersibles to investigate deep-sea life.

Scuba diving over a coral reef

AUV *Artemis* is designed to examine polar ice.

Research ships

New research vessels are being designed to do studies at sea. These large ships are stocked with essential tools for specific investigations, such as studying underwater rocks, offshore oil rigs, polar ice, or creatures of the deep.

Autonomous underwater vehicles

Robots that travel underwater without a human driver are called autonomous underwater vehicles (AUVs). They are programmed on land before being sent on special missions to collect scientific data from the oceans.

Research ship *Neil Armstrong* is named after the first man on the moon.

Snorkellers can discover sea life close to the water's surface.

Snorkelling

Simple snorkelling equipment has made it possible for anyone to see marine life wherever they choose to swim. The mask gives a clear view underwater, while the tube stretches above the surface so that the snorkeller can breathe.

Sea supplies

Oceans support the lives of people all around the world, and provide opportunities for transport and trade. Their waters are full of natural resources, and food and ingredients for medicines can be found beneath the waves. Fossil fuels, such as oil and gas, lie under the ocean floor.

Propeller-like blades are turned by the power of the wind.

Offshore wind turbines

Wind turbines in the oceans catch strong sea winds. The power from the spinning blades is changed into electricity using a generator. This makes renewable energy (energy that does not run out when used) without using up other resources or polluting the oceans.

Minerals

Over time, the natural processes taking place in undersea rocks produce different minerals, such as salt, magnesium, and titanium. Marine mining is usually carried out along the coast, to reduce the cost and the damage to the environment.

Seaweed

The largest supplies of seaweed are grown off the coast of Asia – China is the world's leading producer. Seaweed farmers collect this marine plant to sell as food or as an ingredient for medicines.

Fish

Fish can be caught using many different methods. Traditional fishing involves using small boats and nets. However, bigger trawlers (fishing boats) can drag large nets along the sea floor to scoop up fish and shellfish in huge amounts.

Ocean cargo

Cargo ships can carry more weight than aircraft, while using less fuel. They can transport all types of supplies across the oceans in hundreds of box-shaped containers.

Cargo ship packed high with containers

ossil fuels

and natural gas are located deep inside layers
rocks under the ocean floor. They can be reached
drilling. The largest offshore oil fields and gas
erves are found in the Persian Gulf, in the
ddle East. Fossil fuels are not renewable.

Under threat

Today, the world's oceans are in danger. Scientific research shows that human activity is polluting the waters, damaging ecosystems, and destroying wildlife. New laws are being introduced to preserve the oceans and protect the creatures that live there before it is too late.

Fishermen drag in a huge catch of fish from a trawler.

Overfishing

Large trawlers (fishing boats) are emptying the oceans of fish. This means that some groups of fish, such as the Atlantic bluefin tuna, are at risk of extinction.

Antarctic minke whales caught by a Japanese whaling ship

Oil spills

This bird, called a cormorant, is stuck in a layer of oil. Oil spills from ships pollute the waters and poison wildlife.

The Great Pacific Garbage Patch

Ocean currents have trapped huge amounts of litter and waste in the North Pacific Ocean. Known as the Great Pacific Garbage Patch, this area is bigger than the USA, and mainly contains plastics as they do not wear down naturally.

Triggerfish swimming in a sea of plastic

Whaling

The whaling trade has dramatically reduced global whale populations. There are strict rules to limit whaling, but whales are still hunted for their meat, oil, and bones.

Chemical waste in Morocco is dumped into the Atlantic Ocean.

Pollution

Every day, human activity creates sewage, chemicals, and other waste, which end up dumped in the oceans. This is extremely harmful to marine animals and their habitats.

Climate change

The planet is getting hotter. Oceans, coastal cities, and underwater ecosystems are suffering from the harmful effects of climate change. Global warming is mostly caused by people burning fossil fuels and chopping down forests, which damages Earth's atmosphere.

Drowning islands

The Funafuti atoll is a ring of islands in the Pacific Ocean. Rising sea levels are causing these islands to sink. Scientists think that Funafuti may completely vanish within the next 50 years.

Waves crashing against Funafuti atoll

Melting glaciers

Since the 1900s, the higher temperatures caused by global warming have made glaciers melt faster than ever before. The extra water has resulted in rising sea levels, more floods, and less ice for animals who depend on it to survive.

Coral bleaching

Warmer water temperatures can cause corals to release crucial algae from their bodies. The corals then turn white in a process called coral bleaching. Over time, corals die and entire ecosystems can be lost.

Rising sea levels

As huge ice sheets melt, sea levels rise around the world. Coastal cities, such as Miami, in the USA, Amsterdam, in the Netherlands, and Shanghai, in China, are at risk of flooding. In the future, the effect of flooding on these areas could be devastating.

Ocean acidification

Oceans are becoming more acidic and less salty because of rising levels of carbon dioxide gas in Earth's atmosphere. This result of climate change is called acid bath, and it can damage marine ecosystems and be deadly to some sea creatures.

On thin ice
The ice sheets in Antarctica and Greenland are melting, which is one of the reasons for rising sea levels. In the Arctic, walruses and polar bears live on the ice, but it is disappearing quickly.

Ruined reefs
The world's largest coral reef is the Great Barrier Reef in Australia. However, two-thirds of this reef is now damaged by coral bleaching. This is devastating for all the sea creatures who depend on coral reefs for their survival.

Flood risk
Bangladesh already has regular flooding. By 2050, the sea level is expected to rise by 50 cm (20 in). This could see Bangladesh lose about 11 per cent of its land and pose a threat to nearly 15 million people who live in low-lying coastal regions.

Catastrophic coral
These coral reefs in the South China Sea are dying. Acidic waters are harmful to most shellfish, so there are fewer crabs and lobsters. This disrupts the ocean food chain as many creatures eat shellfish.

Meet the expert

We put some questions to Chloe Harvey, an ocean conservationist who is a Director of The Reef-World Foundation. She travels to coral reefs around the world and teaches people how to protect them.

Q: Why is ocean conservation so important?

A: We can thank the oceans and the creatures who live there for every breath we take. Our oceans are the support system for everything we need to survive. The health of life in our oceans is under threat from increasing temperatures as a result of a changing climate, overfishing to feed a growing global population, and because habitats are being destroyed by human activity. In order to keep enjoying the lives we live and the beauty of our blue planet, we must take action to look after marine life.

Q: What do you love most about the oceans?

A: Its magical powers! I am lucky enough to have been a scuba diver since I was 12 years old. Every time I plunge beneath the waves, I enter into a silent and calm world filled with adventure, colour, and magnificence.

Q: What is a typical work day for you?

A: Every day is completely different. I am one of only five full-time staff at The Reef-World Foundation, which means that we all need to do a bit of everything to keep the organization running. As well as travelling to exotic destinations and developing our global programmes, I also spend a lot of time in rainy Britain, sitting behind a computer writing reports and working on our accounts.

Scuba diving near a coral reef

Q: What tools do you use in your job?

A: Since I started my work with Reef-World in 2009, I have always believed that education is the most valuable tool to inspire the change we need to preserve our oceans. I enjoy listening to all the wonderful and passionate people I have the honour of working with – from the leader of a Philippine village and a rubbish collector in Malaysia, to national political leaders. They have taught me all I know, and I see it as my responsibility to pass on their messages and lessons to others.

Education is necessary to help protect the oceans.

Q: What are your hopes for the future of ocean conservation?

A: That the children of today are given the chance to do things better than previous generations. I'm driven by the words and actions of kids today who are demanding change to turn the tide on global warming and the destruction of our natural world. We know what we have to do and it's time to start doing it.

Write a letter to your local politician, educate your parents, or make your own ocean-friendly choices. You can make a difference.

Q: Do you have any tips for how we can clean up our oceans?

Chloe has pledged to stop using plastic straws in her drinks.

A: Each of us can make small changes to the way we live our lives. We can replace our clothes less often, use fewer chemical cleaning products in our homes, buy fewer plastic products, and eat less meat. Over time, technology and products that are more ocean-friendly will be more easily available.

Q: What is the best thing about your job?

A: To work with the most incredible team and to know that every step, every success, and every minute I spend working will help to protect precious marine life in the sea.

Q: What is your favourite sea creature?

A: The wunderpus octopus – the master of disguise. This octopus can change its appearance in the blink of an eye, from a regular octopus to a slithering black and white striped sea snake, to a dancing sea feather, or to a flat fish lying on the sea bed. To confuse a predator, trick its prey, or maybe just for fun, this incredible octopus is the ultimate fancy dress champion!

Protecting our oceans

There has never been a more important time to protect the oceans. The combined threats of fishing, plastics, and pollution are harming the seas as never before. International governments, conservation groups, and local communities are working together to keep the oceans safe.

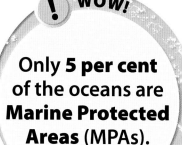

! WOW!

Only **5 per cent** of the oceans are **Marine Protected Areas** (MPAs).

This fish farmer is using a cast net.

Sustainable fishing

Overfishing happens when too many fish are caught too quickly. Sustainable fishing is the opposite of overfishing. It protects fish populations and lets them breed to produce more fish. Using special equipment, such as cast nets and spears, means that fish can be caught without harming the environment.

Marine reserves

Some areas of the ocean are Marine Protected Areas (MPAs). In these zones, it is illegal to fish or to build. MPAs provide protection to fragile underwater ecosystems and encourage new types of sea creatures to grow.

Wrangel Island in the Arctic Ocean is an MPA.

Cleaner seas

In 1972, the United Nations Environment Programme started. Their "Clean Seas" campaign is an agreement by 57 countries to reduce the amount of plastic polluting the oceans and to encourage recycling.

These volunteers are cleaning up a beach in Bangladesh.

These shelters keep people away from newly hatched turtles.

Caring for coastlines

Coastlines are protected so that people and wildlife can live in harmony. Marine animals and coral reefs must not be disturbed if they are to survive. At the same time, local communities need protection against the risks of erosion (land wearing away) and floods.

Helping out

Each and every one of us can play a part in protecting the oceans. Clearing litter from beaches, using fewer plastic products, and choosing to eat sustainable seafood are all good ways to help protect the environment.

People gather together to clean up coastlines.

Oceans facts and figures

The world's oceans are full of fascinating features and marvellous marine creatures. Here are some weird and wonderful facts and figures you might not know.

The **total weight** of **Antarctic krill** in the oceans is **greater** than the total weight of the **human population** of the world.

The **ice sheets** in the **Arctic Ocean** are **shrinking** by **8 per cent** every **10 years**.

200 volt

The torpedo ray can produce a 200-volt electric shock, which is enough to kill a small fish in an instant.

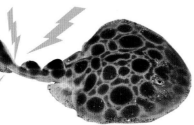

19,794

The Pacific Ocean is about 19,794 km (12,300 miles) wide, which is more than five times the diameter of the moon.

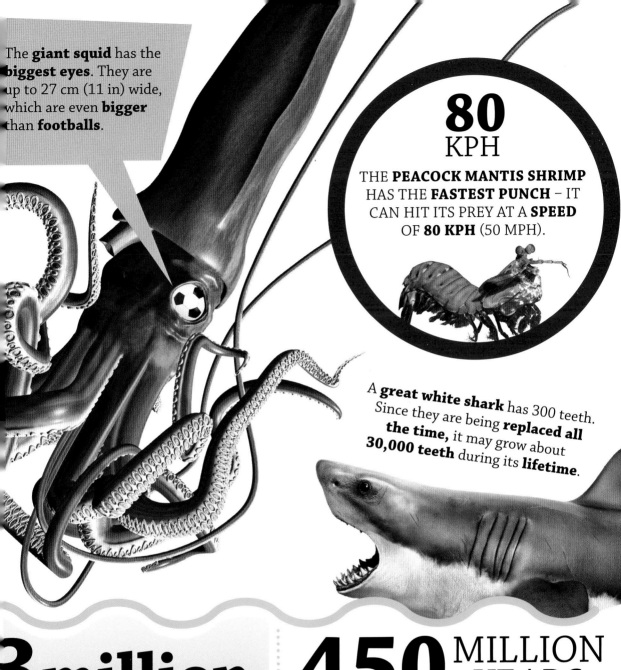

The **giant squid** has the **biggest eyes**. They are up to 27 cm (11 in) wide, which are even **bigger** than **footballs**.

80 KPH

THE **PEACOCK MANTIS SHRIMP** HAS THE **FASTEST PUNCH** – IT CAN HIT ITS PREY AT A **SPEED** OF **80 KPH** (50 MPH).

A **great white shark** has 300 teeth. Since they are being **replaced all the time,** it may grow about **30,000 teeth** during its **lifetime**.

3 million

here are 3 million shipwrecks across e world's oceans.

450 MILLION YEARS

Starfish have lived in the oceans for almost 450 million years – long before the first dinosaurs lived on Earth.

450 million years ago

181–169 million years ago

 # Glossary

Here are the meanings of some words that are useful for you to know when learning all about oceans.

absorb To take in something

adapt When an animal or plant becomes better-suited to its habitat. For example, a penguin's thick feathers keep it warm in icy places

algae Simple, plant-like organism that is found in or near water. Seaweed is a type of algae

bacteria Tiny living things

basalt rock Type of rock found on the ocean floor

bathyscape Type of submersible

bioluminescence Chemical reaction in which an animal produces light

blubber Thick layer of fat in some animals, such as whales; it protects them from the cold

breed To produce offspring

camouflage Patterns or colours on an animal's skin that help it blend in with the environment

cargo Goods carried on board a ship

chasm Deep crack in the ground

climate Weather patterns for a specific area

climate change Process of Earth's climate changing over time

colony Group of animals who live together, such as seabirds

conservation Protecting an area on Earth, such as the oceans

coral reef Huge rocky structure, which has grown gradually from the skeletons of tiny sea creatures

decibel Unit that measure the loudness of sound, whe silence is 0 decibels (dB)

dorsal fin Fin located on the back of a sea creature, such as a shark

ecosystem Living community of plants and animals found together, and their environment

environment Surrounding in which an animal lives

erosion Breaking down of rock by wind and water

evaporation When water heats up and turns into water vapour

flooding When a river or the sea overflows and fills land with water

fossil fuel Type of energy that is not renewable, such as oil

fresh water Water that is not salty, such as rivers, ponds, and most lakes

glacier Large mass of ice that moves slowly down a slope

global warming When worldwide temperatures rise

‎‎itat Natural home of animal or plant

‎a Red-hot, melted rock t flows out of a volcano en it erupts

‎-lying land Land that ear to the sea level

‎mmal Warm-blooded mal with a backbone that skin covered in hair and ds its young milk

‎rine Describes animals t live in the sea, their itat, and environment

‎gration Regular group vement of animals, often feed or breed, or for safety

‎nerals Substances that living things need in ler to grow

‎eanographer Person who dies oceans and seas

‎otosynthesis Process at green plants use to ke food

‎ison Harmful substance eased by an animal or nt that may be deadly couched or eaten

‎edator Animal that hunts her living animals for food

prey Animal that is hunted for food

remote Far away from another place, or difficult to get to

renewable Energy or fuel that will not run out when used, such as wind power

scuba Device that allows the wearer to breathe underwater

sea ice Ice that forms when ocean water freezes

shoal Large group of fish who swim together

streamlined Smoothly shaped to move easily through water. Sharks are streamlined, which helps them swim fast

submersible Boat or vehicle that can travel underwater, such as a bathyscape

sustainable Able to continue or be supported for a long time

tectonic plates Giant slabs of rock that make up the Earth's crust

vessel Boat or ship

voyage Journey to a place, usually by boat or ship

water vapour Gas that is made when water is heated

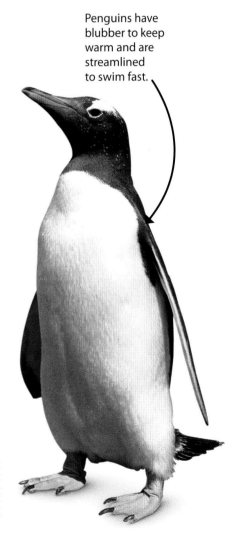

Penguins have blubber to keep warm and are streamlined to swim fast.

Index

Acknowledgements

The publisher would like to thank the following people for their assistance in the preparation of this book: Dan Crisp for illustrations; Aishwariya Chattoraj and Katherine Marriot for design assistance; Kathleen Teece for additional editorial; Becky Walsh for editorial assistance; Polly Goodman for proofreading; Helen Peters for compiling the index; Chloe Harvey for her "Meet the expert" intervie and The Reef-World Foundation for the photographs on pages 54–55.

The publisher would like to thank the following for their kind permission to reproduce their photographs:

(Key: a-above; b-below/bottom; c-centre; f-far; l-left; r-right; t-top)

1 Alamy Stock Photo: Helmut Corneli (b). **2 Alamy Stock Photo:** Nature Picture Library (crb); NOAA (br). **2–3 Getty Images:** Mark Newman (bc). **3 Alamy Stock Photo:** blickwinkel (bc). **Dreamstime.com:** Peter Van Dam (tr). **naturepl.com:** Bryan and Cherry Alexander (crb). **4–5 123RF.com:** Iakov Kalinin. **4 Dreamstime. com:** Etherled (bc). **5 Alamy Stock Photo:** Sean Pavone (tr). **Dreamstime.com:** Askme9 (bl); Ddkg (tc). **6 Dreamstime.com:** Onepony (clb/Choppy); Alex Scott (clb). **iStockphoto.com:** Merrillie (bl). **7 123RF.com:** Inacio Pires (tl). **Dreamstime.com:** Michael Pelin (tr). **8–9 Dorling Kindersley:** Ed Merritt. **9 Dorling Kindersley:** Ed Merritt (cla). **10 Alamy Stock Photo:** Solvin Zankl (fcr). **Dreamstime.com:** 111camellia (c); Harvey Stowe (cra). **11 Alamy Stock Photo:** Nature Picture Library (fcl); Kelvin Aitken/VWPics (ftl); NOAA (tl); Paulo Oliveira (cl); Science History Images (cr). **Dreamstime.com:** Ppaula09 (cla). **FLPA:** Norbert Wu/ Minden Pictures (c). **Getty Images:** Corey Ford/Stocktrek Images (tr). **Science Photo Library:** British Antarctic Survey (tl). **13 Alamy Stock Photo:** Science History Images (cb, crb). **Dreamstime.com:** Jinyoung Lee (cb/ Sea Anemone). **14 Dreamstime.com:** Barbarico (cr); Thelightwriter (bl). **15 Alamy Stock Photo:** Tsado (cra). **Getty Images:** Peter Johnson/Corbis/VCG (clb). **16 Alamy Stock Photo:** AGAMI Photo Agency (bc/Emperor Penguin); Arterra Picture Library (c). Dreamstime.com: Sergey Korotkov (bc). **17 Alamy Stock Photo:** Christian Musat (b). **Dreamstime.com:** Sergey Uryadnikov/Surz01 (tc); Vladimir Seliverstov/Vladsilver (c). **18–19 naturepl. com:** Bryan and Cherry Alexander. **19 Depositphotos Inc:** Pixabay: JChristophe_Andre (c); Unsplash: Annie Spratt (cr). **20 Alamy Stock Photo:** All Canada Photos (crb); Jon Sparks (cl/warship); Ian Dagnall (tl). **Dreamstime.com:** Nongnuch Lerdniyomchon (cl). **20–21 Dreamstime.com:** Sirirak Kaewgorn (Background). **21 Alamy Stock Photo:** Jan Butchofsky (crb); FLHC 3 (cl); Sportsphoto/20th Century Fox/ AA Film Archive (t). **Dorling Kindersley:** Natural History Museum, London (cr). **22 Alamy Stock Photo:** blickwinkel (bl). **iStockphoto.com:** Michael Zeigler (cl). **23 Alamy Stock Photo:** imageBROKER (cla); Seaphotoart (bl). **Dreamstime.com:** Krzysztof Odziomek (tr). **iStockphoto.com:** Eduardo Baena (cr). **24 Alamy Stock Photo:** Juergen Ritterbach (crb). **Dreamstime. com:** Peter Van Dam (cl); Daniel Poloha (cra). **iStockphoto.com:** CoreyFord (tr). **25 123RF.com:** natchaphohn (t). **Alamy Stock Photo:** blickwinkel (clb); Natural Visions (tl); YAY Media AS (r). **Dreamstime.com:** Tom Linster (bc). **26 Alamy Stock Photo:** Reinhard Dirscherl (cr); imageBROKER (tr). **Dreamstime.com:** Dirk Jan Mattaar (bl). **27 Alamy Stock Photo:** Helmut Corneli (crb); Reinhard Dirscherl (l). **Dreamstime.com:** Allnaturalbeth (tr). **28 Alamy Stock Photo:** Nature

Picture Library (br); WaterFrame (bl); Paulo Oliveira (cr). **29 Alamy Stock Photo:** Peter Mc Cabe (b); Dennis Frates (tl); Helmut Corneli (cl, cr). **30 Alamy Stock Photo:** Adrian Sherratt (br). **NASA:** (cl). **31 Alamy Stock Photo:** Eye Ubiquitous (tl); David Fleetham (tr). **32 Alamy Stock Photo:** imageBROKER (clb); Nature Picture Library (cl); Stephen Frink Collection (crb). **33 Alamy Stock Photo:** Mike Hill (clb); Steve Jones (crb). **Dreamstime.com:** Inge Blessas (cla); Gary Parker (tr). **34 Alamy Stock Photo:** Max Allen (bl); Danita Delimont Creative (br). **35 Alamy Stock Photo:** blickwinkel (br); Krisken (bl). **Getty Images:** Westend61 (b). **36 Dreamstime.com:** Standret (bl). **iStockphoto.com:** MWP (cl). **37 Dreamstime.com:** Karlosxii (c); Jesse Kraft (tc). **Pixabay:** LuisValiente (bc). **38–39 Alamy Stock Photo:** WaterFrame. **39 Alamy Stock Photo:** Amar and Isabelle Guillen - Guillen Photo LLC (tr); Ian Bottle (c); Hemis (cr); Stephen Frink Collection (bc). **40 Alamy Stock Photo:** Ethan Daniels (cb); National Geographic Image Collection (tl). **Getty Images:** Dave Fleetham (clb). **Robert Harding Picture Library:** Jürgen & Christine Sohns (c, bc). **40–41 Alamy Stock Photo:** National Geographic Image Collection (ca); Nature Picture Library (c). **41 Alamy Stock Photo:** age fotostock (cr); Wildestanimal (tc, c); Nature Picture Library (bl); WaterFrame (br). **Dreamstime.com:** Linda Bucklin (tr). **42 Getty Images:** Mark Newman (b). **iStockphoto.com:** GeorgePeters (cl, c). **43 Alamy Stock Photo:** National Geographic Image Collection (cla, ca); Nature Picture Library (c, cr). **Getty Images:** Seanscott (b). **44 Alamy Stock Photo:** AF archive (cl); Granger Historical Picture Archive (cl); National Geographic Image Collection (cra); Alain Le Garsmeur Dr Sylvia Earle (cr). **44–45 Dreamstime.com:** Rangizzz (Background). **45 Alamy Stock Photo:** INTERFOTO (tc); ZUMA Press, Inc. (cl); Science History Images (cr). **Scott Taylor Photography Inc.:** (cra). **46 Getty Images:** Henry Groskinsky/The LIFE Images Collection (cl); Twins (r). **47 Alamy Stock Photo:** US Navy Photo (cr). **Dreamstime.com:** Denis Moskvinov (bl). **Getty Images:** LSIS Bradley Darvill/Australia Department of Defence (tl). **48–49 123RF.com:** Iakov Kalinin (b). **Dreamstime.com:** Zoom-zoom (Background). **iStockphoto.com:** Pareto. **49 Alamy Stock Photo:** Joerg Boethling (tr); FORGET Patrick (cr). **Depositphotos Inc:** MasterMariner (clb). **Dreamstime.com:** Arthur Franklin (c); Pradeep Raja Kannaiah (cl). **50 Alamy Stock Photo:** Jeffrey Rotman (clb). **50–51 Alamy Stock Photo:** Jeremy Sutton-Hibbert (bc). **Getty Images:** Mike Hill (t). **51 Alamy Stock Photo:** Paulo Oliveira (cra). **iStockphoto.com:** Cmturkmen (bc). **52 Alamy Stock Photo:** Global Warming Images (bl). **52–53 Alamy Stock Photo:** Howard Chew (b). **53 Alamy Stock Photo:** Peace Portal Photo (t); Helmut Corneli (ca). **Getty Images:** Mamunur Rashid/NurPhoto (cb). **56 Getty Images:** Yuri Smityuk\TASS (br). **iStockphoto.com:** Blackholy (cl). **57 Alamy Stock Photo:** David Pereiras (br); Muhammad Mostafigur Rahman (tr); PhotoStock-Israel (cl). **58 123RF.com:** natchaphohn (cra). **Dreamstime.com:** Astrofireball (br). **FLPA:** Fred Bavendam/Minden Pictures (bc). **59 Alamy Stock Photo:** Helmut Corneli (cra); Paul Fleet (l). **Depositphotos Inc:** Morphart (br). **Dreamstime.com:** Mark Turner (crb).

60 123RF.com: Inacio Pires (tl). **61 Dreamstime.co** Sergey Korotkov (br). **62 Alamy Stock Photo:** Natic Geographic Image Collection (tl). **64 Alamy Stock P** Sportsphoto/20th Century Fox/ AA Film Archive (tl)

Endpaper images: Front: **Alamy Stock Photo:** WaterFrame crb; **Dreamstime.com:** Adfoto bc, Lanaufoto cla, Neirfy clb; **Getty Images:** Raimund Linke cra; Back: **Alamy Stock Photo:** Oliver Denker Reinhard Dirscherl c (Reef), imageBROKER cl, Luis Lea cr, Mauritius Images GmbH c, br, Paulo Oliveira bc (Sp whale); **iStockphoto.com:** ByronD bc.

Cover images: Front: **Alamy Stock Photo:** blickwir fcra, Helmut Corneli cra, imageBROKER bc, Stephen Frink Collection l, YAY Media AS cla, crb; **Dreamstime.** Dirk Jan Mattaar cr; Back: **Alamy Stock Photo:** imageBROKER tr; **Dreamstime.com:** Peter Van Dam Tom Linster cr; Front Flap: **Alamy Stock Photo:** Mike br/ (2), Christian Musat cb, Nature Picture Library c (Lobster), cr; **Dreamstime.com:** Nongnuch Lerdniyom bl/ (2), Ppaula09 ca; **Getty Images:** Mark Newman cra (2), Twins cra; Back Flap: **123RF.com:** Kajornyot cr; **iStockphoto.com:** Naumoid tc

All other images © Dorling Kindersley
For further information see: www.dkimages.com

My Findout facts:

Ocean records

Highest-jumping fish

Key features

The thresher shark can jump 6 m (20 ft) out of the water.

This shark has a very long tail to swipe and stun small prey.

Most dangerous animal

Key features

More than 5,000 people have died from box jellyfish stings.

The venom contains about 200 different chemicals.

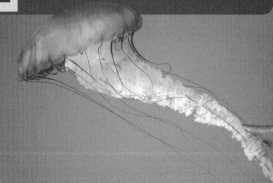

Deepest depth

Key features

The deepest point discovered on Earth is the Mariana Trench.

It is 11 km (7 miles) below the surface of the Pacific Ocean.

Fastest fish

Key features

The sailfish can swim at speeds of up to 110 kph (68 mph).

This ocean predator uses its long bill to tear into shoals of fish.